Community Helpers

Helping After Disasters

by Trudy Becker

FOCUS READERS
PIONEER

www.focusreaders.com

Focus Readers is distributed by North Star Editions:
sales@northstareditions.com | 888-417-0195

Produced for Focus Readers by Red Line Editorial.

Photographs ©: Shutterstock Images, cover, 1, 4, 8, 11, 12; iStockphoto, 7, 15, 17, 18, 21

Library of Congress Cataloging-in-Publication Data
Library of Congress Cataloging-in-Publication Data is available on the Library of Congress website.

ISBN
979-8-88998-014-8 (hardcover)
979-8-88998-057-5 (paperback)
979-8-88998-141-1 (ebook pdf)
979-8-88998-100-8 (hosted ebook)

Printed in the United States of America
Mankato, MN
012024

About the Author

Trudy Becker lives in Minneapolis, Minnesota. She likes exploring new places and loves anything involving books.

Table of Contents

Chapter 1

A Storm Hits

A huge **hurricane** rushes through a city. Waves crash into buildings. A strong wind whips. The storm is very dangerous. People try to find safe places to stay.

Later, the storm ends. The water flows away. But the problems are not gone. The city needs help. Some people get paid to help. It is their job. But **volunteers** can help, too.

Did You Know?

Some volunteers come from nearby areas. Others come from far away.

Chapter 2

Food and Water

After disasters, people need some things right away. They need food. They also need water. These needs are **urgent**. People can't live without them.

Volunteers hold **food drives**. Some people collect food. Others help deliver it. Clean water is also important. Volunteers can bring it to the area. They make sure it goes to the people who need it.

Did You Know?

Volunteers should listen to **community** members. They can hear what kind of help is needed.

Chapter 3

Rebuilding

Some volunteers help **rebuild**. After disasters, buildings are often ruined. Some people might need new homes. Others might have lost their place of work.

Volunteers can help fix broken buildings. They might help build new ones, too. Before this happens, **architects** can help make plans.

Did You Know?

Rebuilding schools is one kind of **long-term** help.

Giving Blood

Sometimes people are hurt in disasters. They might need extra blood. So, volunteers can **donate** their own blood. Health care workers collect the blood and store it. Then, doctors can use it. They can help people who are hurt.

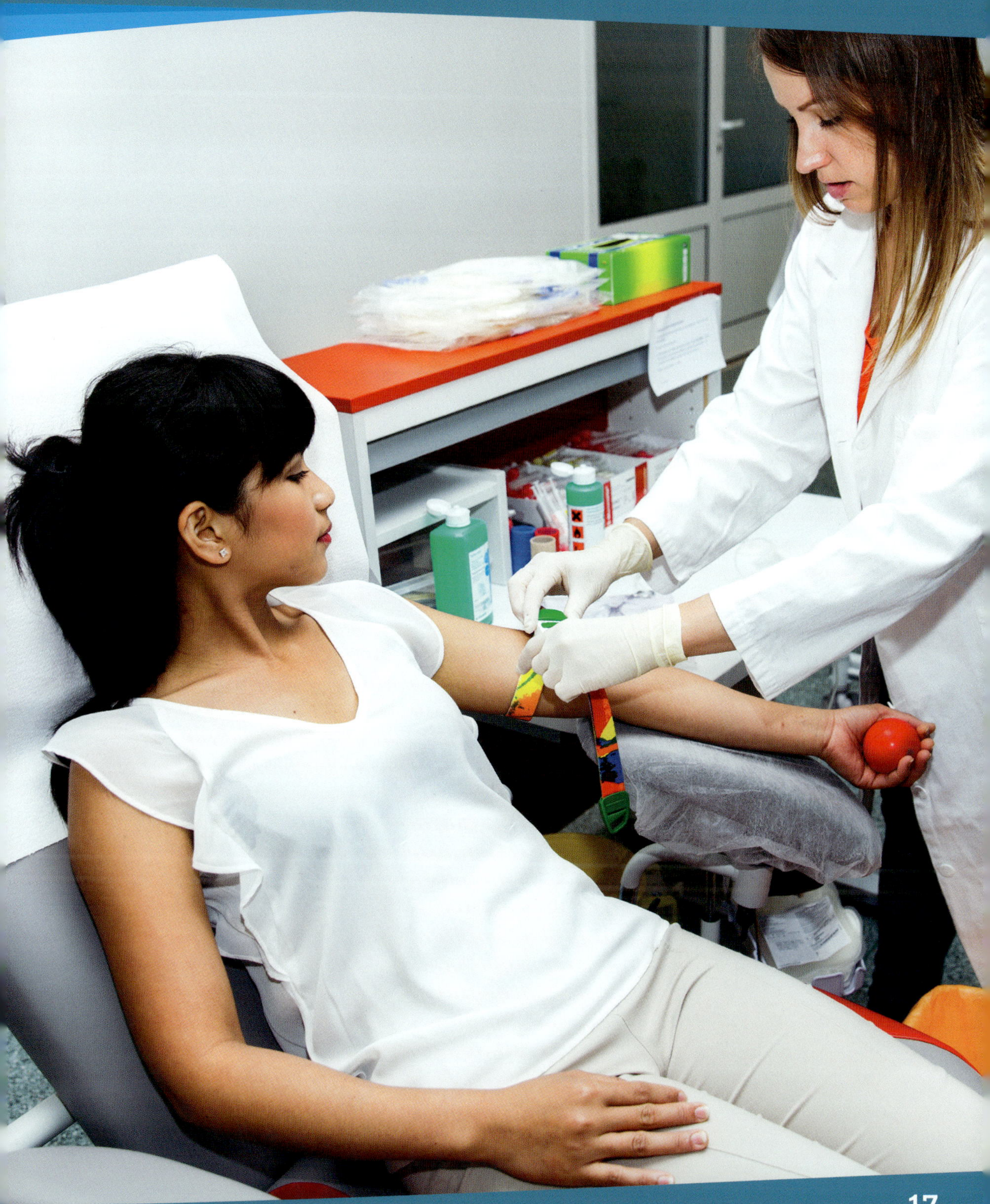

Chapter 4

Other Ways

People can help after disasters in other ways, too. People can donate money. It's used to pay for more help. Or people can send things like clothes or blankets.

Sometimes people can't donate. They can't rebuild, either. But they can still help. They can spread information about the disaster. Then, others can learn about it. Those people might be able to help.

Did You Know?

Some volunteers offer their homes. People with no home can stay with them for a while.

FOCUS ON

Helping After Disasters

Write your answers on a separate piece of paper.

1. Write a sentence that explains the main idea of Chapter 2.
2. If you were in a disaster, what kind of help would you want? Why?
3. After a disaster, which needs are most urgent?
   A. books and blankets
   B. food and water
   C. new buildings
4. Which action is a type of rebuilding?
   A. giving blood
   B. donating money
   C. fixing homes

Answer key on page 24.

Glossary

architects
People who create plans for making buildings.

community
A group of people and the places where they spend time.

donate
To give something away to people in need.

food drives
Events where people collect food to give away.

hurricane
A dangerous storm with strong winds and heavy rain.

long-term
Over a long period of time.

rebuild
To build things again.

urgent
Needing help or attention right away.

volunteers
People who help without being paid.

To Learn More

BOOKS

Miller, Marie-Therese. *The US National Guard in Action.* Minneapolis: Lerner Publications, 2023.

Rossiter, Brienna. *Hurricanes.* Mendota Heights, MN: Apex Editions, 2023.

NOTE TO EDUCATORS

Visit **www.focusreaders.com** to find lesson plans, activities, links, and other resources related to this title.

Index

Answer Key: **1.** Answers will vary; **2.** Answers will vary; **3.** B; **4.** C